THE LONG ROAD
FROM SUFFERING
TO GLORY

CANON ANDREW WHITE

Big
Canon
Books

Published by Big Canon Books

email: admin@canonandrewwhite.com

www.canonandrewwhite.com

British Library Cataloguing in Publication Data

A catalogue record for this book is available from the British Library

ISBN: 978-1-916586-00-0

Design and Print Management by Verité CM Ltd
West Sussex UK

www.veritecm.com

Dedicated to the triumph of Emily Purple
In the midst of suffering, true glory exists.

The long road from '"SUFFERING TO GLORY" is inspired
by my dear friend Emily Yeskoo, pictured on this book.
She was literally the person who suffered more than any
other young person I have ever known. She had a serious
cerebral disease could not move, talk, eat or drink. I met
her through her father who was a US diplomat in Iraq with
me. He was one of my close Wheaton College friends.

I asked one night in chapel for people to talk about
prayers they had not had answered and he told the story
of his dear daughter Emily. I started to visit her in their
family home in Canada. She really did grow to be one of
my closest and most inspirational friends. I spoke at her
funeral when she finally left for glory.

THE LONG ROAD FROM SUFFERING TO GLORY

It always disturbed me that all my glory days had been in Iraq. It was only when I sat down and started work on this book that I realised that my days of supernatural power and glory had indeed not begun in the Promised Land. My days of the supernatural had really begun when I was a student at St Thomas' Hospital. It was there that I became an active member of St Mark's Kennington and came under the ministry of Nicholas Rivett-Carnac, Jean Darnell and Colin Urquhart; they really were the people who taught me to live in the supernatural.

However, my glory days really began big time when I was in Israel doing my first theological doctorate on theologies of Israel. I remember becoming great friends with an Ultra-Orthodox Chasidic Rabbi S (I don't say his full name). I learnt two of the most important lessons of my life from him. The first was that you could not learn about Judaism at the Hebrew University, and I needed to go to Yeshiva. I ended up being the first Goy I have ever met who went to an Ultra-Orthodox Yeshiva in Mea She'arim.

The second was about glory. He made clear that there was no way I could understand theologies of Israel unless I first understood the glory of Israel. He took me aside and whispered to me as if he was telling me a secret. Indeed, it was a big secret for this person was not a only a Jew but a believer in Jesus. His secret whisper got worse: it was not just a secret believer, but a woman called Sister Ruth Ward Heflin. Ruth Heflin was known far and wide around the world as the Great Glory Lady. She ran something which was then called the Mount Zion Fellowship.

Ruth Heflin was a larger-than-life character both physically and spiritually. She made up very holy and spiritual songs, and had a very deep, loud voice. Being involved in their worship always involved a radical move from the physical to supernatural glory. What became clear to me very soon was that there was indeed a very major glory dimension in this Israel work. It took a while for me realise that there was great similarity between the Ruth Heflin glory movement and the early radical charismatic movement of the early Chasidic movement and of its founder known as the Bal Shem Tov (the Good and Holy Name).

What developed was my supernatural understanding of Heflin and Hasidic glory. People look at these Ultra-Orthodox Jews as if they are just bound to their study of the Torah and Talmud, but they are not. They are in fact the radical charismatics of the Judaic movement. Once I was on the inside of the movement it was a different world, one that I was falling in love with by the hour. The highlight of the week was the *"tish"*, Yiddish for "table". After a vibrant Friday-night meal, all the Yeshiva students would descend on Rebbe's table. There would be serious charismatic worship, prayer and dancing. Every person present would then get a blessing from the Rebbe and eat some bread left over from his plate. It is considered a great mystical blessing to celebrate with the Rebbe, who is seen as the closest person to HaShem, the Almighty.

It was Friday 4th February 2022. With major Jewish influence on my life, it is quite traditional for me to go shopping on Friday afternoon and this day I went shopping as usual. I had found the morning quite difficult emotionally. What I was struggling with was the fact that I was now paraplegic and could only use one arm. I can cope with not being able to walk but not being able to use both arms was very difficult for me to cope with.

When I got to the checkout it suddenly dawned on me that the man in charge of the checkout was in fact also paraplegic. It was incredible how he managed the checkout with only one working arm. He did everything with a great smile on his face. When I had got through the checkout, I said to him, "I am so proud of you; you are obviously paraplegic, but you manage your job so well. Thank you for encouraging me so much."

He smiled at me and said how much he appreciated what I had said. I was not wearing my clerical collar so there was no way that he could have known who I was. He told me that his name was Matthew and that he was a member of Hammer Church. Without knowing who I was he started to tell me that Canon Andrew White had even been to his church. I told him that I was Canon Andrew White and his shock and amazement were incredible. I was thinking G-d does not just work in the Middle East; he can even work in the leafy and affluent south of Britain. All I could do was say, "Thank you, Lord, that your wonder and glory is everywhere."

MEETINGS AND MEMORIES

The lockdown had by now affected a major part of my life. It was 2020. Most of my life was spent in the Middle East. Mainly between Jerusalem, Jordan and Baghdad. Prior to ordination and Cambridge I studied and worked as an operating department practitioner at St Thomas' Hospital, which was part of the University of London. I eventually specialised in anaesthetics and I rapidly fell in love with the subject. My main interest was not just putting people to sleep but raising them up. My final responsibility was running the crash team dealing with cardiac arrests. It was this job that enabled me to have a wonderful life as a real adrenaline junky. It was indeed this job that equipped me with the ability to deal with urgent crises in the middle of war zones.

Most of my life post Cambridge and ordination had been based in Jerusalem, until G-d very clearly sent me to Iraq. The story is told in depth in my previous books. To move from Jerusalem to Babylon was not the way it was meant to be. I did not want it but I did it, and it took over my life. I ended up spending nineteen years in the heart of Babylon. Iraq became my home, and it was not long before I began to see myself as a Baghdadi. The people became my people, their language became my language, and their church became my church. It was a totally intimate relationship and I loved it.

Until 2014 I led the largest church in Iraq – St George's, Baghdad. The Archbishop of Canterbury had basically told me that Baghdad was getting so dangerous that if I stayed I would be killed. He continued to say that I could do more for my people if I was alive than if I were dead. I had to agree with him so reluctantly moved to Jordan. Many of my Iraqis, who were scared for their lives, moved soon after me to Jordan. We rapidly realised that we needed a school for our children so within weeks we founded the establishment of a large school for Iraqi refugee children. The school grew to take on a central role in our substantial ministry now in Jordan.

So much of my life has been very painful – I mean physically, mentally and spiritually. Throughout my teen years I suffered many years of very serious illness. I had a very serious form of lymphoedema and had continuous surgery to try and deal with various aspects of the condition. The pain was excruciating but the main aspect of these years of suffering was not the agony of surgery but the horrendous situation that occurred every time I developed septicemia. However, the worst and most painful experiences of my life were not connected with the pain of the surgical problems of my youth; they were more to do with the problems I had faced in my life since I was diagnosed with MS.

I will never forget the day I was diagnosed – 3rd November 1998. I had been very unwell in hospital for six weeks, where I'd been given a lumber puncture and was waiting for the results of the analysis of my CSF (cerebrospinal fluid) to come back. Sure enough they came back, and the diagnosis was positive. What happened next was my first major experience of the journey from suffering to glory.

9

My wife Caroline was in the final stages of her pregnancy. It may have been brought on by my diagnosis, but sure enough Caroline was soon in labour and that evening our second son was born. From being diagnosed with MS to having my dear little Jacob born, all on the same day, I have often said was the beginning of a life of agony and ecstasy. This was indeed the real beginning of my long journey from suffering to glory.

I HAVE BEEN KIDNAPPED, TORTURED . . . BUT THEN CAME COVID

I have recently told the story of the majesty of the Lord literally in the war zone, in my book *Glory Zone in the War Zone*. It has been a great story. I continue to do my work in areas of great trauma despite the recent pandemic. Everything changed when I was admitted to hospital near my home in England. Despite struggling with the battles against MS for many years, what I was now fighting was very different and far harder. I was diagnosed with Covid and was in hospital for eighteen weeks. It was a very hard situation. The various medical conditions have been nothing compared to the extreme isolation that everybody went through, as patients weren't allowed to even meet any of their family. Despite being in a very busy place, it was a very lonely time.

What I saw in the Covid Zone is a place and glory like never before. The divine supernatural stories in this Covid Zone were endless.

My treatment was basic nasal oxygen therapy and intravenous antibiotics but then the doctor came to me with a major life-and-death decision they wanted me to make. Did I want to be ventilated if normal breathing stopped? I had made the decision in the past – many times in my medical days – that certain patients were not for resuscitation. When you make the decision about yourself it is very different. At the same time, it is very liberating knowing that on all accounts everything is in the hands of the Lord Almighty. So I was clear: I did not want to be ventilated or resuscitated. The doctor agreed that was the right decision.

My consultant neurologist trained in Liverpool, but I noticed his name was Issa Ibrahim. He noticed that I was taking great interest in his real name on his badge. My interest was not just because he had a Christian Arab name. I knew there was something else. I looked at him and said, "Do you know me?" He smiled at me and said, "I just so happen to have been one of your Sunday school children in Baghdad when I was ten." He could not believe that he was in Guilford talking to one of his patients in Aramaic, the ancient language of Jesus uniquely used by Christians in Iraq.

I had another incredible encounter with my physiotherapist Gauda. It turned out that she was not just from Jordan but her whole family lived in the very same road as me in Amman. This was a real G-d-given opportunity. For me, this time of desolation was only made better when one of the night nurses turned out to have spent twelve years working in Israel. I cannot but see this as the supernatural provision of the Almighty that in this Covid time I could speak all my usual languages of Arabic, Aramaic and Hebrew. What this Covid time has assured me of is that our Lord is always with us, even in the most difficult times. I had said to G-d, "If I am to survive this time of total isolation, I must be able to speak these ancient Semitic languages," and suddenly I was with those caring for me who spoke those languages.

I tell of some of the supernatural stories of my post-Covid medical care, well, the fact is throughout all my many years of suffering G-d has always been there. The time before the Covid crisis I actually became very ill when I was speaking at my spiritual home of Bethel, Redding, California. The night after preaching I rapidly became very ill with acute abdominal pain. What's more, by the morning I was also beginning to show significant signs of sepsis: hyperpyrexia, tachycardia and hypotension. I had already had these slight worrying symptoms earlier in the week.

That morning, whilst in acute pain we thought about how we could get me to the ER. We simply prayed, "Come, Lord Jesus, come." Sure enough, Jesus came in the form of a supernatural Bethel doctor called Mercedes. She could see immediately that I needed to be admitted to hospital and promptly arranged for an ambulance to transfer me to the very hospital and ward where she was working. Despite being in a terrible physical state I immediately knew that I loved her. Over the days, once drugged up on serious opioids and IV antibiotics, I realised there was more in common with us than I had originally thought. Not only was she a Spirit-filled medic like me, she was also a serious Sabbatarian. That means, like me, she was also serious about keeping the real seventh day holy as the Sabbath.

So, spiritually and academically we remain close friends to this day. She is also serious about reconciliation, and we very much hope we may be able to work together in the future. Just as our Lord so powerfully provided for me in my medical crisis, so will he provide for you and your loved ones in their crisis.

The major challenge to me post hospital was how I was going to continue to work. My physio, who had been visiting me at home, made it clear that I would not be well enough to get back to the Middle East for quite a while. I love Ulster, Northern Ireland, so was delighted when a group of Ulster clergy contacted me to say they wanted to work with us and support us. Still so upset that I could not go to Ulster, I was amazed when I was contacted by Alee and Angus, two young people I had met on a previous Ulster visit. When I saw them, I felt G-d tell me these two people were meant to get married, so I told them I would come over and take their wedding. They contacted me and said, "We are getting married in a few weeks. Will you come over and take our wedding?" I had promised years ago that I would and suddenly my desperate desire to go to Ulster had been met.

The one issue that has always been central to my memories has been my love for Israel and my love for the Palestinians. As I write it is Jerusalem Day – the day in 1967 when Jerusalem was reunited. A great day for Israelis, a tragic day for Palestinians, many of whom lost much. I love and work with both communities, and I will continue to do so. I will be attacked by both sides but I will not stop loving them both. This is the land of the Holy One. The Six-Day War happened between 5th and 10th June 1967 but the date it happened was 28 Iyar 5781 and it is that day today as I write. Due to the fact that they keep the Jewish calendar it does not match up with the Western Gregorian calendar.

I had not been working long on this "Meetings and Memories" chapter when the Israeli/Palestinian conflict blew up again big time. It was the greatest escalation in the conflict since 2014. It was suggested by many that I should return. Having just come home from my eighteen weeks in hospital with Covid I knew that I was in no fit state to make such a venture. My international chairman and senior colleague Chief Rabbi Michael Melchior was on the ground and I knew that he was the only one with the knowledge and wisdom of Israel and Hamas who could bring about real negotiations to bring about a ceasefire.

Negotiations were intense on both sides. Long into the night there were meetings and discussions. By day nineteen of the conflict there began to be some real signs of hope. The negotiations did not just involve people on the ground but also other key Arab nations such as Saudi Arabia and Egypt.

What this whole traumatic experience has taught me is that my influence matters and can have a serious positive effect even when I am not on the ground.

This chapter on memories I feel should really contain my true but most painful memories. People know in part but only very vaguely about the most difficult and painful aspect of my ministry. I feel that this is the right time for me to seriously tell of the trauma related to what happened resulting in my final resignation from the Foundation for Relief and Reconciliation in the Middle East (FRRME).

In 2014 the terrible news was revealed about ISIS taking women and girls mainly from the Yazidi community and using them as sex slaves. What was happening to these poor females is just too awful to mention but I feel the story must be told.

I did manage to get some of the girls back but at no time did I pay money to terrorists. It just so happened that the people who had kidnapped me years before, I only got myself out by promising to get some of their leaders out of American detention, which I managed to do. Little did I realise that years later it would lead to my demise with the Charity Commission. They carried out a full enquiry into us. Fortunately, they never closed our charity down but did forbid me from being a charity trustee or dealing with any of the money.

I gave away lots of money but it was not charity money; it was all mine personally from endowments and inheritance, resulting in many tens of thousands of pounds. Sadly, much of this money recently has been used to pay for the care of my wife and I as we have both seriously deteriorated since MS, followed by a radical demise with Covid. One year later I am still requiring daily professional care. None of this is paid for by social services, with the exception of the district nurse who deals with all issues relating to my catheter.

The good news is that despite all of our problems we are still managing well. Sadly, since my Covid illness I have had few preaching or teaching engagements, thus our charity income has gone down resulting in our medical and dental clinics in Jordan having to close. We hope and pray we will be able to reopen them soon.

The first real preaching engagement I had in the year since having had Covid was at one of my favourite churches, Cornerstone in Walton-on-Thames. The pastor said that the glory was there big time and that he could see physically the Holy Spirit's glory surrounding me. I was so aware that when I was there, I was ministering in the same level of glory that I did in Iraq. For so long I have been asking G-d to see his glory like I did in Iraq. He just kept saying, "It is coming soon." When I was in the midst of the Sunday service, I felt the glory returning for the first time. I knew that G-d had said to me that through the Covid tragedy the glory would return.

Pastor Chris Demetriou came up to me after the service and said he had seen the glory of G-d surrounding me like a halo. Yes, it had been a tragedy, but it had also been a time of great glory. We are expecting that this time of glory will truly lead us onto the next exciting stage of our ministry.

The Covid pandemic did not just hit the USA and UK but the whole world and all the places where I work, especially Israel, Iraq and Jordan. Over 80 per cent of our families in Jordan were infected. Israel had a major vaccination onslaught and the country became clear very quickly.

People rejoiced, became jubilant and stopped protecting themselves – within days Israel was terribly infected again. The Delta variant of Covid soon became the dominant strain in Israel so the lockdown in Israel returned.

Meanwhile, I remained in England and despite the lockdown having been partially lifted, it made no difference to me. I still only saw the same three people walk past my window each day. The private estate I live on I christened fifteen years ago the "most boring estate in the world" has not changed its portfolio one iota.

My personal recovery from Covid-19 has been a slow and long, drawn-out process. This virus sure is real and difficult. I may have been one of those who was sceptical about the reality of the pandemic originally but once you've had the reality of the full-blown illness you cannot deny it. Every day I pray, "Lord, what are you teaching me through all this?" All I can hear and think is "patience" and I am not very good at that. So, it has been a good learning experience.

I ask myself continually, "Have I really learnt what I was supposed to learn?" and I think I am not sure. So I list now the issues I know I must explore further. As I write I have not learned it all (past tense), but I know that I am learning (present tense). Here are five points which I want to explore:

1. **Patience**
2. **Glory**
3. **Victory**
4. **Power in Weakness**
5. **Shalom and Peace**

1. Patience

By its very nature patience is not something I find easy. I have said before that from my early medical days when I chose to work on the cardiac arrest team I have existed as an adrenaline junky. I literally spent my time running from one medical crisis to another.

When I finally arrived in Baghdad as a peace negotiator, I often say I learnt more doing my job at St Thomas' Hospital than I did in the academic halls of Cambridge reading Theology. The learning was something I was first introduced to through my education in Ignatian and Benedictine spirituality. We all need to be patient in the way we listen to and engage with our Creator. Being struck down by Covid radically taught me I had to find another way. I could no longer live a radical, do-it-all life.

My time in hospital was a radical time of me accepting that patience was something I needed to learn and endure. There were times I when could do nothing; at one point I could not even see. No longer could I even use my left arm or leg. I had suffered many of these problems before but after Covid it was at a totally different level. Learning patience in this situation was not something I could slowly learn and meditate on; it was simply a survival mechanism.

2. Glory

My next major lesson that I had to learn in my terrible Covid experience was how to move into glory. I had been spending so much time preaching and speaking about glory; it had been at the very centre of my life. I had just written a book called The Glory Zone in the War Zone. To me the Glory Zone was always talking about the glory of heaven coming to earth. It was the supernatural becoming real in my life. It meant praying for the sick and seeing them radically healed in front of me.

One of my favourite chapters in my glory book is on "The Presence of Angels in our Midst". Worship in the war zone creates a higher zone of glory and literally attracts the angels. We saw them most during times of worship. Angels were there to instruct, guard and protect – and many times we even managed to capture images of the angels on camera. I love to talk about the angels, and I talk in the book about how whatever war zone you may be in – political, economic, relational or physical – with Jesus, you can know the reality of a heavenly Psalm 91- Zone. A zone where you experience his presence surrounding you and his angels encircling you.

There is not just one word for glory in scripture. In the Hebrew Scriptures the most common word used for glory is *"kavod"* which simply means "heaviness". Glory is seen as a heavy, real, physical and tangible presence of the Almighty. It really is heaven come down to earth.

In New Testament Greek the word used most to describe glory is *"doxa"*, which is where the word "doxology" comes from. The word most commonly used to describe glory is *"shekinah"* (correctly pronounced Shehinah). It is a word not actually found in the Hebrew Scriptures or the New Testament but it comes from the intertestamental Jewish book, the Targum. Here it also refers to the physical presence of the Lord making himself known when he appeared as the fiery furnace when Moses came down from Mount Sinai.

In the long, hard, desperate place when I was literally dying of Covid, I so wanted to experience G-d's glory, but I could not. I had been in desperate situations before when my very closest friends were being killed all around me, but never had I been void of G-d's glory. Now I was thrown into glory-less darkness. In a lifetime of religious diplomacy this was by far my worst ever experience.

In my suffering I could not even read the Bible, therefore I just recited to myself passages that I knew well and that had been part of my life in the most difficult of times. My central passage on hope and glory was from one of the least-known minor prophets, Habakkuk.

> I heard and my heart pounded, my lips quivered at the sound; decay crept into my bones, and my legs trembled. Yet I will wait patiently for the day of calamity to come on the nation invading us. Though the fig tree does not bud and there are no grapes on the vines, though the olive crop fails and the fields produce no food, though there are no sheep in the pen and no cattle in the stalls, yet I will rejoice in the Lord, I will be joyful in God my Saviour. The Sovereign Lord is my strength; he makes my feet like the feet of a deer, he enables me to tread on the heights. (Habakkuk 3:16-19)

As I looked at the end of my glory section of this book, I certainly could see how I had moved from the Covid Zone to the Glory Zone but, as you will see, it was hard, so very hard. This is so often the case when we go through dark and terrible suffering. We know that in the midst of terrible and frightening darkness, glory will eventually break through despite the journey being long and hard.

3. Victory

After patience and glory in the Covid Zone I come to victory. I do not have any easy solutions to suffering but what I do have is the certainty that there is no victory without first enduring the pain. As we look at the story of Jesus, we see that his greatest victory came after his greatest suffering. Only after his death on the cross did we see his final victory. Only then did we hear the final victory cry: "IT IS FINISHED."

In my Covid state I could not see a time for my final victory cry, but I knew it was coming. With the major pandemic lockdown my life and ministry could not function in the way that it used to. The only news was Covid. Suddenly I was plunged into the heart of the subject: I had full-blown Covid. I now had something relevant to the major crisis of the moment. I am not saying that G-d caused me to go down with this virus, but I am saying that despite everything, G-d gave me the victory in ways I would never have thought possible. I now could talk into the very heart of the crisis. I had been there and suffered much but had the victory. My talks now had a new relevance in the time of the crisis. Despite all the pain and suffering, I survived.

So many good friends who were far fitter than me did not survive. I conquered it and had the victory. It is not falling that is so bad, it is not getting up. That is my victory message: yes, I fell but I got up again and I am ready to see even greater victory now. My victory cry is simply, "Hallelujah! I have conquered." I have conquered and have the victory because he, my Maker and Creator, helped me get back up when I fell.

Ultimately, victory is the Lord's and not mine. It is a victory that I will carry with me in the years to come. As with our Lord, death is vanquished. I am alive and he has the victory.

4. Power in Weakness

So much of my story so far demonstrates the fact that the whole scenario of me coming down with Covid radically reduced the power that I thought I had. When I talk of power, I am talking about the basic strength I had to function. Yet I realised that despite this major loss of strength, I had maintained my ontological power. I had lost my physical strength, but my emotional strength began to return. I still had my vision. I knew without doubt that my primary call was to support and help sustain the persecuted church. I knew that by G-d's grace he had enabled me to be part of the persecuted church for many years.

I had been shot at, kidnapped, persecuted, yet I knew for a fact that my strength had been made perfect in weakness. I still managed to carry out an international ministry whilst in the natural being very ill. I knew for certain that I had the joy of the Lord deep down in my heart. That joy of the Lord is there for us all. So, whatever your crisis – be it depression, broken relationships or illness – look deep down in your heart, and you will find that joy.

5. Shalom and Peace

I said that the final reason I was going to give for me surviving Covid was shalom and peace. There is no better day to look at this response than on *erev Shabbat* (the Sabbath eve). Shabbat, the day of true peace given as a gift of G-d. I was conscious in hospital I always managed to keep the Sabbath. Shabbat is truly a great gift of G-d and the one day when you should stop "doing" and just concentrate on being in the presence of our Divine Creator. I may be a Christian not a Jew, but I have always been a Christian that has taken Shabbat very seriously. I try and observe it as much as I can. To me, even when was very ill, Shabbos was still the day when I could stop worrying about "doing" and could just concentrate on being in the presence of Hashem.

Shalom is, in essence, the very backbone of my work. Reconciliation is about making peace where people thought it was impossible. This is my passion and driving force in life. Knowing that this is my passion and knowing that my work has only just begun was what forced me to keep going.

As I write we are entering Shabbat in the last month of the Jewish year. Elul is traditionally a time of introspection and stocktaking – a time to review one's deeds and spiritual progress over the past year and prepare for the upcoming "Days of Awe" of Rosh HaShanah and Yom Kippur

As the month of Divine Mercy and Forgiveness (see "Today in Jewish History" for Elul 1) it is a most opportune time for *teshuvah* ("return" to G-d), prayer, charity, and increased *Ahavat Yisrael* (love for a fellow Jew) in the quest for self-improvement and coming closer to G-d. Chassidic Master Rabbi Schneur Zalman of Liadi likens the month of Elul to a time when "the king is in the field" and, in contrast to when he is in the royal palace, "everyone who so desires is permitted to meet him, and he receives them all with a cheerful countenance and shows a smiling face to them all".

Specific Elul customs include the daily sounding of the *shofar* (ram's horn) as a call to repentance. The Baal Shem Tov instituted the custom of reciting three additional chapters of Psalms each day, from 1st Elul until Yom Kippur (on Yom Kippur the remaining thirty-six chapters are recited, thereby completing the entire book of Psalms).

Having looked seriously at the five points in depth, which really sustained me through this most traumatic period, I cannot deny how much I gained from these five weapons of spiritual survival; weapons in a time of great crisis. What is clear is that each of these responses had a profoundly spiritual dimension to it.

What was becoming clear by the day was that I was not just dealing with a serious personal illness but a massive pandemic. I have had so many of my friends and colleagues infected. My PA became positive, then my youngest son. Meanwhile friends were not just getting the virus but some have even died. These have been friends literally all around the world, not just in the US and UK but throughout the Middle East, Iraq, Turkey, Pakistan and Bangladesh. Added to the Covid problems there was a huge fire that raged through Turkey, the place where a large number of our Iraqis are now resident.

What is clear is that we faced an almost apocalyptic crisis. All we can do is pray, "Come, Lord, we need you."

Since writing my last paragraph everything has changed. The Taliban have overtaken Afghanistan. It may not be a country I myself have been based in but many of my team have. The Iraqi and Afghan team were basically one and the same. We worked together, we lived together, we suffered together. When the Americans withdrew several weeks ago, I said categorically that this would lead to an all-out war with the Taliban. People objected to what I was saying but it was true. The risk to all, including the UK and US, is great. The only good thing is that people have moved away from just thinking about Covid and are now thinking about some of the bigger issues of international security.

My return to the Glory Zone from the Covid Zone has seriously been hindered by being pulled into the Afghan Taliban Zone. Though I have not worked there myself, many of my former Iraqi colleagues have worked there both as diplomats and in the military, and were basically all doing very similar jobs.

Since the Taliban are all Muslim, it is easy for people to say it is Islamic terrorism. It is not. It is simply terrorism.

Every religion has terrorists. The one thing they all have in common is that they are all evil. It does not matter what religion they are, the fact is that when religion goes wrong it goes very wrong. That is what is happening: these people are all desperate for more power. They will use radical and evil means to gain that power. They want control and influence. We must not get caught up in religious bigotry. The answer is simply to love, love and love those who are most difficult to love – after all, we are all told to love our enemies.

My concern with my desire to avoid any link with Islamophobia in no way takes away from my strong personal Christocentric position. My life and work is totally connected to my work and calling as a minister of reconciliation. The very nature of my work is related first and foremost to the Abrahamic religions as my work is predominately in the Middle East. I have utmost love and respect for those I work with. I am very conservative in my faith tradition and do not even believe in interfaith worship, though I do think I can participate in Jewish worship.

FROM A COVID ZONE TO THE GLORY ZONE

Today is one those days that in Arabic we would call *yom basal* (an onion day). A day when everything seems to be going wrong – health problems, Caroline problems and work problems, not to mention world problems. Yet in all these problems we know we are more than conquerors. That our Lord is in total control and that his will is that *yom bassal* (onion day) will become *yom assal* (honey day). The Arabic term *yom assal, yom bassal* was a regular term of our daily vocabulary in Iraqi life. A term I confess I regularly use in my English vocabulary.

As I continue my slow recovery, I must confess that I am showing intense symptoms of slow- or long-term Covid. My physical state is so much worse than when I was previously just recovering from a flare up of MS. My neurological function is considerably worse; I am now basically hemiplegic. My left leg never worked well but now my left arm and leg fail to move at all. I used to touch-type well but now I can only type with my left hand, which means that writing a book takes so much longer. Praise G-d I can still do it just as I always have; it just takes so much longer. And as I have already said, it takes so much more patience. I know without doubt that more glory is coming – I don't know how or when, but I know it is.

This journey out of the Covid Zone today is reminding me of Shadrach, Meshach and Abednego after they had been captured by Nebuchadnezzar and thrown into the fiery furnace. Daniel chapter 3 tells the full story.

The Image of Gold and the Blazing Furnace

King Nebuchadnezzar made an image of gold, sixty cubits high and six cubits wide, and set it up on the plain of Dura in the province of Babylon. He then summoned the satraps, prefects, governors, advisers, treasurers, judges, magistrates and all the other provincial officials to come to the dedication of the image he had set up. So the satraps, prefects, governors, advisers, treasurers, judges, magistrates and all the other provincial officials assembled for the dedication of the image that King Nebuchadnezzar had set up, and they stood before it.

Then the herald loudly proclaimed, "Nations and peoples of every language, this is what you are commanded to do: As soon as you hear the sound of the horn, flute, zither, lyre, harp, pipe and all kinds of music, you must fall down and worship the image of gold that King Nebuchadnezzar has set up. Whoever does not fall down, and worship will immediately be thrown into a blazing furnace."

Therefore, as soon as they heard the sound of the horn, flute, zither, lyre, harp and all kinds of music, all the nations and peoples of every language fell down and worshipped the image of gold that King Nebuchadnezzar had set up.

At this time some astrologers came forward and denounced the Jews. They said to King Nebuchadnezzar, "May the king live forever! Your Majesty has issued a decree that everyone who hears the sound of the horn, flute, zither, lyre, harp, pipe and all kinds of music must fall down and worship the image of gold, and that whoever does not fall down and worship will be thrown into a blazing furnace. But there are some Jews whom you have set over the affairs of the province of Babylon – Shadrach, Meshach and Abednego – who pay no attention to you, Your Majesty. They neither serve your gods nor worship the image of gold you have set up."

Furious with rage, Nebuchadnezzar summoned Shadrach, Meshach and Abednego. So, these men were brought before the king, and Nebuchadnezzar said to them, "Is it true, Shadrach, Meshach and Abednego, that you do not serve my gods or worship the image of gold I have set up? Now when you hear the sound of the horn, flute, zither, lyre, harp, pipe and all kinds of music, if you are ready to fall down and worship the image I made, very good. But if you do not worship it, you will be thrown immediately into a blazing furnace. Then what god will be able to rescue you from my hand?"

Shadrach, Meshach and Abednego replied to him, "King Nebuchadnezzar, we do not need to defend ourselves before you in this matter. If we are thrown into the blazing furnace, the God we serve is able to deliver us from it, and he will deliver us from Your Majesty's hand. But even if he does not, we want you to know, Your Majesty, that we will not serve your gods or worship the image of gold you have set up."

Then Nebuchadnezzar was furious with Shadrach, Meshach and Abednego, and his attitude toward them changed. He ordered the furnace heated seven times hotter than usual and commanded some of the strongest soldiers in his army to tie up Shadrach, Meshach and Abednego and throw them into the blazing furnace. So these men, wearing their robes, trousers, turbans and other clothes, were bound and thrown into the blazing furnace. The king's command was so urgent and the furnace so hot that the flames of the fire killed the soldiers who took up Shadrach, Meshach and Abednego, and these three men, firmly tied, fell into the blazing furnace.

Then King Nebuchadnezzar leaped to his feet in amazement and asked his advisers, "Weren't there three men that we tied up and threw into the fire?"

They replied, "Certainly, Your Majesty."

He said, "Look! I see four men walking around in the fire, unbound and unharmed, and the fourth looks like a son of the gods."

Nebuchadnezzar then approached the opening of the blazing furnace and shouted, "Shadrach, Meshach and Abednego, servants of the Most High God, come out! Come here!"

So Shadrach, Meshach and Abednego came out of the fire, and the satraps, prefects, governors and royal advisers crowded around them. They saw that the fire had not harmed their bodies, nor was a hair of their heads singed; their robes were not scorched, and there was no smell of fire on them.

Then Nebuchadnezzar said, "Praise be to the God of Shadrach, Meshach and Abednego, who has sent his angel and rescued his servants! They trusted in him and defied the king's command and were willing to give up their lives rather than serve or worship any god except their own God. Therefore I decree that the people of any nation or language who say anything against the God of Shadrach, Meshach and Abednego be cut into pieces and their houses be turned into piles of rubble, for no other god can save in this way."

Then the king promoted Shadrach, Meshach and Abednego in the province of Babylon.

A wonderful story of the triumph of the G-d of light and hope over evil. This is the triumph of the angel of light and hope over demonic destruction. At the very heart of all of our callings in this difficult zone is the call to be a people of faith. We know that we only need faith as small as a mustard seed to throw a mountain into the sea. One of my favourite passages on faith comes from Hebrews 11:

Now faith is being sure of what we hope for and certain of what we do not see. This is what the ancients were commended for . . . And without faith it is impossible to please God, because anyone who comes to him must believe that he exists and that he rewards those who earnestly seek him. (Hebrews 11:1,6)

Faith is being sure of what we hope for and certain of what we do not see. Faith is indeed the very heart of what we believe and hope for. We need to have real hope that our faith is destined for something bigger and better. Sometimes we just say, "What, Lord, do you want for me that is bigger and better?" I know what my basic needs are and how they have been so badly affected by being in the Covid Zone.

Through being infected with Covid and MS I have lost everything: health, wealth, vision and influence. They are all very important to me. I may have lost everything, but I have not lost the most important things in my life: my G-d, my Father, my Brother, my Saviour, Lord and King. Throughout this time of total loss, I lost the thing I feared losing the most in life: my vision. But I gained the glory like I had never known it before. For me that was and is the mega Glory Zone.

THE COVENTRY MINISTRY OF RECONCILIATION

Today, as I write, is the twentieth anniversary of the terrible tragedy of 9/11. We all remember where we were when we heard what had happened. I was in my wonderful study in the crypt of Coventry Cathedral. I was just packing my case to fly to Jordan to begin the long and difficult journey to Baghdad. Us Brits are not used to very long journeys, like my American friends are. It was a journey of at least twenty hours for me that was almost unbearable.

As the 9/11 tragedy became known, all international flights were cancelled, and this included my venture. I did not realise it then but twenty years later I can see very clearly how G-d used that terrible event to create, develop and enable my unique ministry to grow a radical ministry of reconciliation in some of the world's greatest danger zones.

The Coventry ministry of reconciliation began in Coventry Cathedral's greatest time of trial, which happened on 14th November 1940 when the German Luftwaffe (air force) carried out one of the earliest major attacks of World War II. The City of Coventry was totally obliterated – its great medieval Cathedral was totally destroyed, being turned into just a ruin.

In the light of the 9/11 tragedy I was looked to by much of the British media as the one who should provide a response to the Twin Towers tragic massacre when over 3,000 people were killed. That was a lot more than the 500 plus killed in the Coventry blitz. One of the things I have learned in my work in disasters is that you must never compare victim numbers. Some may say that the greatest thing to come out of the Coventry blitz was indeed reconciliation. From the beginning of life after the Coventry blitz, the Coventry provost wrote two words on the sanctuary wall – FATHER FORGIVE.

At the time people asked should it not say, "FATHER FORGIVE THEM"?

The provost, Dick Howard, said, "No, we all need to be forgiven. It is not just them."

So eventually the Litany of Reconciliation was formed and became the backbone of the worldwide ministry of reconciliation and remains central to my own ministry and calling. I wrote a book, called *Father Forgive,* which looks at the whole issue of working within the litany of reconciliation.

THE COVENTRY LITANY OF RECONCILIATION

All have sinned and fallen short of the glory of God.
The hatred which divides nation from nation, race from race, class from class,
FATHER FORGIVE
The covetous desires of people and nations to possess what is not their own,
FATHER FORGIVE
The greed which exploits the work of human hands and lays waste the earth,
FATHER FORGIVE
Our envy of the welfare and happiness of others,
FATHER FORGIVE

> Our indifference to the plight of the imprisoned, the
> homeless, the refugee,
> FATHER FORGIVE
> The lust which dishonours the bodies of men, women
> and children,
> FATHER FORGIVE
> The pride which leads us to trust in ourselves and not
> in God,
> FATHER FORGIVE
> Be kind to one another, tender hearted, forgiving one
> another, as God in Christ forgave you.

From this day my life and work changed. No longer was
my work of reconciliation focused on the past; now it
was an issue for the present. It is an urgent issue for now.
Reconciliation post 9/11 is surely a matter of life and death.
So my message for this day is simply FATHER FORGIVE.

YOM KIPPUR

Yom Kippur is the most important day in the Jewish calendar. A day of repentance and forgiveness. Despite not being a Jew I do take the day very seriously and always fast as well. The hardest days of the year for me are always Tisha b'Av and Yom Kippur. I do not use the internet on these two days – for me that is serious fasting.

To keep Yom Kippur is to also keep away from all things of the flesh, including computers, so I do not even post a blog. During the holy day of fasting I meditated much on the normal passages of Lamentation and Jonah (which is one of my favourite books) but I also felt led to meditate on my favourite chapter in the New Testament, which is Romans chapter 8. The verse the Lord drew me to was not the normal passage I so often preach on and meditate on, which is verse 18 talking about suffering and glory, but it was from earlier in the chapter:

> And if the Spirit of him who raised Jesus from the dead is living in you, he who raised Christ from the dead will also give life to your mortal bodies through his Spirit, who lives in you. (Romans 8:11)

Yes, in the natural I should have not survived. I was asked one day by the consultant if I wanted to be resuscitated if I should arrest. I told the doctors not to resuscitate me if I died but I knew that G-d had a different thing for me. It was verse 11 of Romans 8 that ran through my body on the first Yom Kippur since my near-death experience.

As I have always said, it is not falling that is so bad; it is not getting up. If the Spirit of him who raised Jesus from the dead is living in us, he who raised Christ from the dead will also give life to our mortal bodies.

So to my total surprise my Yom Kippur message actually came from the New Testament and Paul's letter to the Romans.

THE PEOPLE WHO KEPT ME GOING

As I think about how I have kept going in really difficult times, whether it be health, work or ministry, it has always been friends and family who have been at the forefront. They are people who have always sustained me in my darkest hour and best hour. Few of them really know how special they are to me. That is unless I have told them that they are in my CLAN. My CLAN are those who are all Called, Loved and Named. They are the people who are the closest to me. Some of them know that they are in my CLAN but many do not. Writing about these people is so important to me, yet I know it might seriously upset people who think they are very close to me but are not listed. Yes, there are other people who are very close to me who I would not see in my CLAN any longer. When I was in Baghdad there was a group called my "inner circle"; they were in essence my CLAN of the day.

The fact is, your inner circle does change over the years. It is sad fact that at different times there are different people who form your closest inner circle but they change and move on. They are still close and important to you but in a very different way. These great friends were a major reason why I came out of the Covid Zone – the people I am, in essence, in love with. Being back with them, even though I do not see them much, is being in the Glory Zone.

I want to share with you briefly my Glory Zone people who I love so much and who really are in the Glory Zone with me.

These are the people who have sustained me through the most difficult of times, both now and in the past.

CAROLINE, JOSIAH (YOSSI) AND JACOB WHITE

My dear wife Caroline, and sons Josiah (Yossi) and Jacob are at the very heart of my life. Sadly, Caroline also developed MS several years after me.

Josiah, our eldest son, went to boarding school while he was in Prep school, then became a day pupil at the Royal Grammar School in Guildford. This is one of the top schools in England and has always finished within the top-ten schools in the country in A-level results. Josiah was able to start at this school earlier than he was supposed to, so he did not have to wait for results of common entry exams.

I had always desired for one of my children to go and study at Cambridge. Josiah passed all his A levels with top marks and therefore got a place to study in Cambridge. I was, of course, overjoyed by this, and when I heard the results I got so excited that I fell out of bed, cut my head open and had to have ten stitches!

Yossi decided not to go to my old college, Clare, but opted to study at Queens' college, famous for being the college with the mathematical Erasmus bridge. I wanted him to originally study Medicine or Arabic but I deliberately did not pressurise him by telling him what I wanted him to do. In the end, he decided to major in Mandarin and Theology.

I had studied Theology in Cambridge and was delighted to see that he had some of my fellow students as his teachers.

Mandarin is the main language in China and therefore very different from Cantonese, which is the main language in Hong Kong. Though there are some similarities, there was in reality very little that we could speak together. I had spent a fair amount of time in Hong Kong and at one point had a fellowship at Hong Kong University. I tried to learn a few Mandarin words but never really developed in the language by far at all.

Three years on from commencing his studies in Cambridge I was delighted to learn that Yossi gained a double first in both Mandarin and Theology. On graduating he returned home to Liphook and was able to get on to a graduate training scheme at Philips, which at that time had its headquarters in Guildford, just twenty miles from where we lived. Yossi's main responsibility was working in the discipline of the maintenance of MRI scanners. This he took great delight in. At one stage he contemplated leaving the company and going to study Medicine as a quick-entry scheme, but he decided to continue with his present work.

Jacob, on the other hand, decided not to go to university but developed other skills, having his own Youtube channel as well as developing various skills in the realm of photography and videos.

I always said that in many ways, Jacob was far more like me than Josiah. Jacob was the high-profile, highly dramatic professional entrepreneur. I would often sit down with the boys and talk about which one was most like me. Yossi decided that he was definitely the one like me because of our academic disciplines. Jacob, who did not go to university, ended up being the highest earner amongst all of us, yet I never totally understood what he was doing. They were both originally attached to the Hillsong Church in Guildford, though, later on, with Jacob relocating to London and Yossi to Brighton, they both became involved with churches that were part of the HTB network — the same network of churches that I had trained in and worked in, in London, before I went to Coventry.

DR BILLY GRAHAM AND WHEATON COLLEGE

I move on from my family to some key people who helped form me to be the person that I am today. Some of these great, great people are not even alive now. The first, who has gone to glory and needs no introduction, is the great Dr Billy Graham. He proved to be such an important person in my life. People often say to me, "How on earth did you get to become such a good friend of Billy Graham?" Well, it was suggested to me by Saddam Husain's office.

Tariq Aziz, Saddam's deputy, asked me if I would contact him. We had taken some senior religious leaders into Iraq. This was when it was totally illegal to visit the country. I was asked if I could take Iraq's top religious leaders to England and America. I told him that I could in England because the Archbishop of Canterbury would help me, but I did not know the leaders in America. Tariq Aziz said there was a very big Christian leader called Billy Graham, and I was to tell him that Saddam Hussain wanted him to invite Iraq's top religious leaders to America. To cut a very long story short, this I did, and it happened.

This was the beginning of a long, wonderful relationship with Dr Billy Graham. It was he who established my substantial relationship with his alma mater, Wheaton College. The college has become a major part of my life over the past two decades. The relationship with Wheaton became particularly strong during my relationship with the US Government and Diplomatic Service in connection with my work in Iraq.

One of the first Wheaton diplomats I got linked with was a wonderful man called Paul Yeskoo. Paul was an active member of my US Embassy Congregation, and we soon became very close friends. Our services were held on Saturday evening, and one Saturday I asked all the congregation to tell me about people who seriously needed our prayers. Paul told me about his dear daughter Emily. Though then in her late teens, she had a serious cerebral illness. This meant that she could literally no longer move, talk, eat or have any cognitive functions. Emily immediately went to the top of my prayer list, and I asked Paul if on my next visit to Canada I could go and see her. This I did, just a few weeks after Paul and I had met. This started a very long and wonderful relationship. Though she was originally born an American, the family moved to Canada where Paul once worked at the embassy. In Canada, medical treatment is given free of charge to all its citizens so the family decided to relocate to Toronto. I would go and see Emily every time that I was in Canada and would often make special trips just to see her.

She really did become one of my closest friends. Literally the only body function she could occasionally manage was to smile and it brought such joy to me to see her smiling. It turned out that whilst the family were based in America, their home was close to the State Department near DC. They attended one of the churches that I regularly spoke at, where many more diplomats and military officers were also involved. Some of them remembered Emily from when she was a little girl and was still able to talk, walk, eat and sing. When I would go back to these churches I would often mention my dear Emily and there would be such a warm response from the young people in that congregation who had literally grown up with her. Wherever I was in the world I would always contact Emily and her mother. And Emily particularly showed great joy when I was worshipping with young people in Baghdad.

They all knew about Emily and real bonds between them and her began to develop. There were times when Emily would deteriorate and go into a very serious medical state and there were other times when she would be taken into a care home so that respite could be provided for her mother Catherine. Eventually, a respite centre was built which they named after Emily and called it Emily's House. It was a great honour for me to officially open the residence in the presence of my dear Emily. She became one of the major features in my life and it was whilst I was at Bethel School of Supernatural Ministry (BSSM) in Redding, California, that Emily went downhill and was taken into hospital.

Within days her function became so bad that she was no longer able to breathe. She breathed her last breath, but even though she was no longer living, she never ceased to be part of my life. It was, therefore, taken for granted that I would be at her funeral, so I flew all the way across to America and up to Canada in order to officiate her truly marvellous funeral service. It was a great day and one I know I will never forget.

So, once again, this all really started through my link with Billy Graham, Wheaton College and the wonderful relationship I formed with Emily's parents. Even though our dear Emily has gone to glory, we continue our relationship to this day. Emily sure was one of my greatest connections with the true glory that I have ever had. And I know that we will meet again one day – not in Wheaton, not in Toronto, but in the ultimate place of glory.

ARCHBISHOP LORD DONALD COGGAN

The greatest inspiration in my life has been Lord Donald Coggan, who was a former Archbishop of Canterbury. I was going to visit a great friend of mine, Clive Marks, one day in Mayfair. We were walking next to each other and Lord Coggan took me by the hand and said to me, "Don't take care, take risks."

That has been my motto throughout my life. He became such a close friend I even introduced my then girl friend

Caroline to him and asked if I could marry her. Fortunately, Lord Coggan and his dear wife Lady Jean Coggan both agreed that Caroline would be a wonderful choice as a wife.

From that day he became a wonderful friend to us both and eventually celebrated our marriage on Easter Monday 1992. There have been many significant events in my life that there were close links to Lord Coggan, even to being awarded an honorary Doctorate in Divinity at his Toronto University, Wycliffe College, where he was once a Professor of New Testament. He took a very deep interest in my work and life and we visited him regularly until he died. He did tell me off, though, for staying in Baghdad in the midst of the major 2003 invasion. He was the one who taught me to take risks, but believed in taking risks carefully. After his death I would also become good friends with his daughter, Dr Ruth Coggan, who spent her life working as an obstetrician and gynaecologist in Pakistan. To this day Lord Coggan remains my greatest mentor and encourager. He taught me to take risks, a lesson I will never forget. Plus, he was also a Cambridge man.

DAVID AND SARAH ARMSTRONG, AND AMELIE

David Armstrong was my total inspiration when I was a student at Cambridge. He was the one who inspired me to spend a life committed to reconciliation. There is no doubt about it that David, with Lord Coggan and Lord Carey, has been the one of the greatest mentors in my life.

David started life as a Presbyterian. This was during a time of the dreadful Catholic/Protestant conflict. There were regular IRA bombings both in Ulster and on the mainland of the UK.

Things for him radically changed when he became friends with the Catholics.

J.JOHN, THE LITTLE CANON

My next great friend of inspiration is the person I call my best friend, J.John, who I first met when I was a theological student at Cambridge. I immediately fell in love with him and thought that one day I would like to be his friend.

It was during my curacy at St Mark's, Battersea Rise, that I had my next opportunity to meet with him. He had been invited to lead a mission. We had a great mission event at Wandsworth Town Hall, where I would one day serve as a councillor. I remember one night when I was preaching on preparing for mission. Caroline was sitting in front of me and I remember thinking, 'I like what I see.' Within days I was going out with her and I immediately got her on the planning group for the J.John mission. So we both became friends with John and his wife Killy.

I can't recall exactly every meeting I engaged with John but what radically became clear was that we functioned as real friends who did everything that we could together and it was not long before we started to arrange our most important event together. John, Killy, Caroline and I would annually go on holiday but I must confess that John and I, who are both total workaholics, would often find a time when we could combine our time of entertainment with work. On one of our holidays to Israel I remember when John and I shot off to Gaza together and met with one of the major Hamas leaders during the time when the second intifada was just getting underway. Our relationship formed with the extremists turned out to be very positive and some of them even joined our peace-making initiatives, which continue to this day.

One of the more enjoyable non-work holidays was when we used to go to the Greek Islands, including Cyprus, which was J.John's original homeland. But Cyprus also proved to be a great place where we could both be involved in ministry and holiday. All of our children – Killy and John have three boys and we have two – used to sometimes go on great holidays together. The relationship became closer and closer.

When I eventually moved to Coventry, J.John was able to carry out his first major *just10* series, which was a series of his inspirational talks on the Ten Commandments. We did some very exciting ventures in that series, which included having big amnesty bins for people to come and drop in any weapon they had, including knives and guns. This venture obviously had to be overseen by the police, who could not quite believe the number of weapons that were being handed over in the cathedral. The *just10* series didn't finish at the Cathedral. It became incredibly successful, taking place throughout the whole country where the combined attendance has exceeded one million people.

One of the things that J.John did was to encourage me to get involved in various churches that he was very active in. Probably the greatest thing I was able to achieve with John was to get him appointed as a lay canon of Coventry Cathedral. At the time he was not ordained and functioned as a super-duper evangelist without any official ordination. It was a great delight when J.John was made a canon non-residentiary of Coventry Cathedral. We immediately started calling each other Big Canon and Little Canon (I was 6ft 4 and he was about 5ft 7). He then began a very successful televised series called *Facing the Canon*, and I was one of his first guests on the show. The venture continues to this day and many high-profile people have faced the canon in this series.

CHRIS DEMETRIOU

Chris Demetriou is one of J.John's great friends; they grew up together in Cyprus and he turned out to be one of the best introductions that J.John made for me to any particular minister.

Since the time when I first met him, which was in the early 2000s, I have visited his church regularly. He has remained a very close friend and one of the biggest supporters of our ministry. Chris Demetriou is now working with us in different aspects of our international ministry and we take great joy in being able to converse on subjects such as Greek and Hebrew. He will help me with Greek understanding and I will help him with Hebrew understanding. This we particularly did when we were doing a series of study on the word 'Glory'.

He continues to be one of my most significant emotional and theological supporters and he and his family are all great friends.

THE CLAN FROM BETHLEHEM

The CLAN from Bethlehem are a wide variety of the young people who all became very close friends after the 2002 siege of the Church of Nativity that I negotiated for. It was at that stage when I asked one of my closest friends, Joseph (the carpenter), what I could do to help his community. He said that the thing they needed more than anything was their very own Syrian Orthodox school. The CLAN are all children who started attending the school, called Mar Ephrem, as soon as it was open. They have now graduated and most of them are students at Bethlehem University. Some are married or engaged. We always have a large dinner together when I am in Bethlehem and started calling ourselves "The CLAN", which stands for "Called Loved and Named".

I'm still very much part of the lives of these wonderful young people. They thought it was rather funny when I went away to Iraq and came back speaking Arabic with a very Iraqi accent. The children are called by their Iraqi abbreviations. There is "Big Nunu", who is Nicola, and there is "Little Nunu", who is Big Nunu's sister Natalie. There's "Juju", who is Juliana, and "Lulu", who is Lara. At the moment, as I write, Israel is still shut off to all visitors due to Covid-19 so I am unable to travel there. I can assure you that when I return, there'll be a major celebration and gathering of the whole CLAN.

MALCOLM MATHEW

Malcolm Mathew is one of my longest-standing friends in life. We became great friends in my very early days at St Thomas' Hospital when we were both students. He was doing his medical school training when I was doing my ODP training. Malcolm used to come and help me regularly in the operating department. We were both very involved in the hospital's Christian Union. One of the funny things about our life together is that he was first with me when I started my early public speaking career.

MY PROMISED LANDS

I am often asked how many different nations have I visited, so yesterday I counted and there are ninety-six that I can remember. Now you probably want to know which ones are my favourites.

At the very heart of my life is my love for Israel and Iraq. Those two have been my Promised Lands. There are two other places that have become like the Promised Land to me. The first is Redding in California, the home of Bethel Church and the Bethel School of Supernatural Ministry (BSSM). The other Promised Land for me is Singapore and the Cornerstone Church, headed by Pastor Yang.

TEACHING AT THE BIBLE COLLEGE IN WALES

I have just spent three days teaching at the Bible College in Wales. It was truly an outstanding experience, one that I will never forget and it was a vital part of my journey from the Covid Zone to the Glory Zone. Being at this college was being at the very heart of the 1904–1905 Welsh Revival for it was started by the great Rees Howells, the revivalist, himself. I may have gone there to teach but I am sure that I gained more than I gave.

I was invited to speak by the great Pastor Yang Tuck Yoong, who is the senior pastor of the Cornerstone Church in Singapore. He bought the college building when it was derelict and about to be destroyed, and then invested £5 million to turn it into the vibrant international Bible college that it is today. I stated earlier that Singapore was one of the most favoured places I had visited in my life. Visiting Pastor Yang and his church was a life-transforming experience. When at his church I was rather surprised to see how pro-Wales this church was. This week all my questions were answered.

Pastor Yang is a major fan of Rees Howells and his total commitment to intercessory prayer. The firm belief is that revival only comes through a total commitment to long sustained intercession. The thing that also runs deep with his commitment to revival was his early love for the establishment of a Jewish people in their homeland of Palestine.

Looking at the history of the Welsh Revival it was amazing to see once again how spiritual renewal of the Holy Spirit meant a new spiritual understanding of the Promised Land, just as we saw at the time of Oliver Cromwell in the Netherlands. Cromwell sent his ministers to Holland to study under Menasseh Ben Israel to learn Hebrew. Ben Israel was a highly charismatic rabbi who not only taught Hebrew but won his students over to passionately believe in the establishment of a homeland for the Jewish people in their historic land. This all came out of a passionate desire to revive the faith.

It is amazing to see that whenever there is a real spiritual revival fervour, there comes with it a new love and belief in Israel and the return of the Jewish people to the Promised Land.

WE THINK IT CANNOT GET WORSE . . . AND THEN IT DOES

It is Wednesday 8th December 2021. I and so many people were hoping that this crisis could not get worse yet today it did. With the development of the new Omicron strand of the Covid virus the prime minister announced that a new major lockdown would come into place. The impact on the whole country – if not the world – is going to be huge. The apocalyptic nature of this crisis is becoming increasingly obvious. Thus the spiritual response to this crisis becomes increasing essential. What is G-d doing and saying? I, like many, do not understand what is happening. This is certainly a time and day of real mystery. Here we are in Advent, which itself is a time of great mystery as we approach the celebration of Christmas.

I thought I had seen the last of the Covid Zone experience but this week I found my self back in hospital again. The same hospital where I had spent four months at the beginning of the year. Ever since my long hospital stay I've had serous bladder problems. I've been catheterised continuously and had serious problems with the catheter. Continually the catheter was becoming blocked and the inflatable balloon in the catheter was bursting, thus not staying in place.

I was therefore admitted to hospital to undergo a cystoscopy to see if there was anything in my bladder that was causing the balloon to be continually cut and thus falling out of place. As usual, I loved being in hospital and being in deep conversation with the various medical and nursing staff.

When I went to theatre I must admit I was slightly nervous about having the procedure done with just topical local anaesthetic, but in the end the procedure worked very well.

No reason was found in the bladder for the catheter laceration. The big problem is that the bladder wall is very thick and is in constant spasm.

Well, the whole venture seemed like just a further extension of the Covid crisis that is effecting the whole world. All the time in this crisis I have been waiting and expecting to see the glory of G-d. I have and do see the glory of the Lord often in the most unexpected of places. Despite all the difficulties, all I can say is that the Lord is here and his Spirit is with me.

As if to really confuse things, we were just approaching Christmas week 2021 and my home-help had found me in a really serious condition. My body was not working and I was feeling as if now my whole world was falling apart and I did not have the help and support I needed. I have been through so many difficult situations in my life and this period was certainly adding to the awful experiences relating to this Covid tragedy. Yet I have always known that G-d had told me that I was to write about the Glory Zone in the Covid Zone. I have seen glory moments in the past year but I know that the true glory is yet to come. All I can do is say, "Come, Lord, in your total glory now."

HOW I REALLY WAS POST SURGERY

Well, my dear friends, it is time for the real news about how I am. The fact is that since my recent bladder surgery and all over Christmas I have been very unwell. However, from today I have seriously improved. My new staff are now all back at work, and we are already working very well together. I am hoping and praying that I will be able to re-start my international travel early in the New Year. By G-d's grace and help I will.

I hoped and prayed so much that my post-Covid time would rapidly move to a glory time. I prayed, believed and hoped but I really went down, down and down. I still pray and hope that the glory will be coming. I have got to believe that the great time and mega glory is coming, and I truly believe that it is.

HAPPY NEW YEAR PAST, PRESENT AND FUTURE

Today I wish all my friends GOY L SHANA TOVA. To be honest I take far more seriously the Jewish new year than the Gentile one. I still look at this new year as a time to look to the past in repentance, the present in acknowledging G-d's supernatural presence, finally it is about our supernatural future in the presence of Ha Shem (G-d in Hebrew). The fact is this new year is a great time for us to reassess where we are in the presence of our Lord G-d.

ANYWAY

In my present traumatic post-Covid state I have been looking at the way that music and worship has been so central in helping me through a very painful and traumatic life. The time of the invasion of Iraq in 2003 was a very traumatic period. My life was helped so much through a CD that was given to me by one of the US Army soldiers. There was a song on it called "Anyway", by the Nashville-based singer Martina McBride. Do listen to this amazing song* and tell me what you think of it. I would love to meet this artist, but I have never met anybody who knew her. It was this song that played constantly through Saddam's palace after he was overthrown.

BECAUSE HE LIVES

The other song that has been vital to my life in times of trauma has been "Because He Lives". It was Easter Saturday in 2004 and I had been up all night that G-d would speak to me about what to say at the morning Easter day service. Suddenly I was overtaken with the words of this wonderful chorus, "Because he lives, I can face tomorrow". A large crowd of staff gathered by the swimming pool and there we all sang those wonderful words. This was such a vibrant service of resurrection. Most of our choir just happened to be military who had previously been students at Wheaton College where I had taught regularly. They reported back to Tony Payne, the director of the conservatory of music who was a very close friend of mine. He phoned me to say that

---

* https://www.youtube.com/watch?v=6uLtyzRgmyI

George and Gloria Gale, who wrote the hymn, were very good friends of his and Wheaton College.

After the worship and sermon, we then moved to the time of baptism. A major part of the coalition was from South Korea. The big general of the Koreans was General Kim. He was not alone; every one of the senior officers also got baptised. So, we baptised the general, the colonel, the captain and sergeant major who were all called Kim, so we had a Kim baptism times four. Ever since then I am often presented with churches singing "Because He Lives".**

NO NEVER ALONE

I was taking the service one evening in the chapel in Baghdad when we started to come under serious attack. Mortars and rockets blasted into the US Embassy, the air-raid alarm started to blast out throughout the Green Zone, there were loud commands to fall face down. Everybody, apart from me, fell face down on the floor but continued to worship, singing:

I've seen the lightning flashing,
And heard the thunder roll,
I've felt sin's breakers dashing,
Trying to conquer my soul;
I've heard the voice of my Saviour,
Telling me still to fight on,
He promised never to leave me,
Never to leave me alone.

** https://www.youtube.com/watch?v=2Oz_caE8oQE

No, never alone,
No, never alone;
He promised never to leave me,
Never to leave me alone.

The song I had never heard before suddenly became the spiritual backbone for me in times of great physical or spiritual battles.

HERE IS LOVE VAST AS AN OCEAN, LOVING KINDNESS AS THE SEA

Here is love, vast as the ocean,
Loving kindness as a flood
When the Prince of Life, our Ransom,
Shed for us his precious blood.

Who his love will not remember?
Who can cease to sing his praise?
He can never be forgotten,
Throughout heaven's eternal days.

On the mount of crucifixion,
Fountains opened deep and wide
Through the floodgates of God's mercy,
Flowed a vast and gracious tide.

Grace and love, like mighty rivers,
Flowed incessant from above
Heaven's peace and perfect justice,
Kissed a guilty world with love.

The next song sum's up so much of who I am now; it also talks about the fact that the good news is not just for where I have come from. I was brought up in a very interesting Christian household. My mother was from a classical Pentecostal background and my father from an ardent reformed Calvinistic tradition. I give thanks to G-d for being part of a very Philo Semitic family. I grew up knowing and loving Israel and believing in its biblical significance. I was brought up knowing about the evils of antisemitism.

THE GOD OF ABRAHAM PRAISE

The God of Abraham praise,
who reigns enthroned above;
Ancient of Everlasting Days,
and God of Love;
Jehovah, great I AM!
by earth and heaven confessed;
I bow and bless the sacred name
forever blest.

The great I AM has sworn;
I on this oath depend.
I shall, on eagle wings upborne,
to heaven ascend.
I shall behold God's face;
I shall God's power adore,
and sing the wonders of God's grace
forevermore.

The heavenly land I see,
with peace and plenty blest;

a land of sacred liberty,
and endless rest.
There, milk and honey flow,
and oil and wine abound,
and trees of life forever grow
with mercy crowned.

The God who reigns on high
the great archangels sing,
and "Holy, holy, holy!" cry
"Almighty King!
Who was, and is, the same,
and evermore shall be:
Jehovah, Lord, the great I AM,
we worship thee!"

I have done a series on the hymns that have greatly helped me on the frontline of the battle. The next song is the simplest and greatest battle song of them all.

JESUS LOVES ME, THIS I KNOW

Jesus loves me, this I know,
for the Bible tells me so.
Little ones to him belong;
they are weak, but he is strong.

Yes, Jesus loves me! Yes, Jesus loves me!
Yes, Jesus loves me! The Bible tells me so.

Jesus loves me he who died
heaven's gate to open wide.

He will wash away my sin,
let his little child come in.

Jesus loves me, this I know,
as he loved so long ago,
taking children on his knee,
saying, "Let them come to me."

MY KEIRA

Many of you may know that I have over fifty godchildren. Following them, praying for them and loving them is one of my great priorities in my life. I recently had a very fine experience when two teenagers, Alexander and Katherine, asked me if I would be their godfather. I said yes and they have both become good friends and I love them so, so much.

Having had godchildren choose me to be their godfather, I decided I wanted to choose my fifty-fifth godchild myself, so I did. There was absolutely no doubt who this should be. There was one young person that I had been in love with since she was born, and that was my Kiera Dulake.

Keira's story is like no other. She was born without a diaphragm. You can't live or breath without a diaphragm. Medical professionals at Southampton University Hospital went to great extents to transfer and transplant muscles from around her body to create this vital organ. I followed her story because both her grandparents worked for us as our gardener and cleaner.

When I think of my dear Keira, I confess I have always thought of her as being mine. From when she was born and was so ill I started praying for her and loving her, and one of my true highlights of her early life was when I went to speak at her primary school wearing all my body armour.

I have met my Keira a few times recently, but it suddenly dawned on me that I really saw her in the same way as I saw my godchildren. I then discovered that she had no godparents so I decided that if she and her family would agree, I would — for only the second time ever — choose a godchild myself. The first was my Amelie in Belfast (who was number thirty-five). She and all her family agreed that this was indeed the right thing to do and finally my Kiera was indeed mine and I love her so much.

She now has a new member of her family and I have a new member of mine. The love we have for each other is not one way but two ways. We loved each other before but now this love has moved to a totally new level. My Keira — number fifty-five — is another glory gift of the Covid crisis. If I had not been so ill for so long, I would not have received this great gift of G-d called Keira. The fact is that if Keira was the one positive thing to come out of this crisis, then it has all been worthwhile. I would not have missed this for anything.

MY RETURN TO THE PROMISED LAND AND I MET WITH AN ANGEL

February 2022 had been an incredible month. I'd been preparing for the important day when, after being in exile for over a year, I'd return to Israel and Jordan, to the real Promised Land. I suddenly understood for the first time what it was like for the people of Israel to spend so long in exile in Egypt. I had spent so long in exile and now I felt just like the people of Israel who were about to move into the Promised Land. This recent time in exile had been such an incredible time of learning about signs, wonders, glory and miracles. I have already shared many of these stories but there will be more to come.

I finally returned to the Promised Land at the end of February. Israel had suffered so much in the pandemic. I had suffered in many ways, like my beloved Israel.

No sooner had I arrived than I was thrown into a highly complex array of meetings. The first meeting involved many of the key people I had worked with for years. Nice people do not cause wars and if you are a peacemaker you have to be willing and able to work with people who have caused wars. As I reflected on our meeting, I gave thanks to the Lord that in our midst was Sheik Imad Fulluji, one of the original founders of the Hamas and the instigator of much violence. Yet through my long-term work with him he had become a major fighter for peace and not war.

My average time of sleeping is never more than four hours. In Jerusalem recently I awoke at 2am. I had been starting my praying by saying to the Lord, "I desperately need your help to raise funds." Since being so ill and the pandemic I had found it almost impossible to raise funds.

At 2.45am I looked at my Facebook messages; there was a message from one of my "friends" who I did not know. She told me that her father, Bishop Paul Lanier, was in Jerusalem, and he would love to meet with me.

By 9 am I was sitting down in the courtyard of Christ Church, Jaffa Gate, having breakfast with him. I immediately knew that this man was a great saint who I had so much in common with – both theologically, politically and regarding Israel we were one. I said, "Thank you, Lord, I have finally met a true partner in Christ," who I knew would be a true partner with searching for glory in both the War Zone and the Promised Land. All I could do was say, "Thank you, Lord."

What's more, he also just happened to be the chairman of the board of the Fellowship of Christians and Jews that I urgently needed to meet with. Yet again G-d had urgently come to my rescue.

WHO ARE MY CLAN?

My CLAN used to be called my "inner circle" in Baghdad days. CLAN stands for being Called, Loved and Named. They are all people who have been like my spiritual children. Some are my godchildren, others are not. They all have a link to the Land of the Holy One and can be Israeli or Palestinian or from the other Promised Land. I love them all so much.

Below is a picture with my Caitlin <insert picture of Caitlin> who is just about to leave high school and join the Israel Defense Forces (IDF). I love my Caitlin so, so much, ever since I first heard her pray at a conference I was speaking at. Her wonderful father, Steve Carpenter, is one of the leaders of the Isaiah 19 Highway movement, the highly prophetic movement that takes seriously the words that talk of the highway of worship and reconciliation from Egypt to Assyria via Jerusalem.

THE MOST INSPIRATIONAL FIGURE I HAVE NEVER MET

As I look back on my immense time of suffering, I am made acutely aware that I have only survived it because of the inspirational people that G-d has put in my life. Most of these people I know personally, like my CLAN, but very occasionally there will be somebody you know and love who you have never met.

For me the one person who falls into that category is Misty Edwards. A truly wonderful and inspiring worship leader with Mike Bickle at the International House of Prayer in Kansas. Like me she has survived life threatening illness, she also loves Israel and is the one person I would so love to meet. So, if anybody knows how I could meet her, please tell me.

DIVINE REVERSAL

At the heart of my life and ministry has been my call to a life of "Divine Reversal". That which was so awful turns around to become the portal of glory. My greatest example of this is how the evil Saddam Hussain was brought down by the USA-led coalition in 2003. I had already been travelling into Iraq regularly for more than five years. Everybody from the British Government and the FCO said it was too dangerous for me to go there. I did, though, because G-d had told me quite clearly that I had to.

Immediately after the takeover of Iraq I was appointed as co-chaplain with the US Army Padre Frank Wismer. Saddam's throne room in his old palace was appointed as our chapel, and his solid gold throne became my pulpit. This was the most perfect example of the scripture in Luke that I have ever seen

> He has shown strength with his arm; he has scattered the proud in the thoughts of their hearts; he has brought down the mighty from their thrones and exalted those of humble estate. (Luke 1:51–52 ESV)

WHO WAS BRIAN THE SQUIRREL

On Tuesday 22nd March 2022, one of my greatest friends, Brian the Squirrel, passed to glory. I want to explain who Brian was and why he was known as Brian the Squirrel.

Brian was a great personal friend and he was a man of very deep faith. He had a very close relationship to G-d but he'd had a rather dodgy past and had even spent time in prison. He worked in the antique trade and owned an antique shop called Squirrel's. Thus, he became known as Brian the Squirrel. The shop had a great array and display of red squirrels.

One day G-d told him to go to the Kurds. He did not even know who the Kurds were. He found out and went to work with the Kurds in Northern Iraq. He grew to love them profoundly. He was involved in every aspect of ministry in Kurdistan. What's more, even though I then became friends with him, I never discovered where or how our friendship began. He knew that I lived near him in England, and he knew I was working in real Iraq (I always called Kurdistan where he worked pretend Iraq). I became a lot closer to him when the trial of Saddam Hussain, Iraq's evil dictator, took place. One of the things Saddam was tried for was the evil massacre of the Kurds, which included the Kurds of Halabja.

To cut a very long story short, I was in Iraq through the trial of Saddam. Once a week I would even fulfil the role as one of the official coalition representatives. On 5th November 1996 Saddam was found guilty of serious crimes against humanity. The High Court Judge Raouf sentenced him to death by hanging. I will never forget the day of sentencing as it was 5th November – Guy Fawkes Day. I can remember thinking that Guy Fawkes was a saint compared to Saddam.

After the trial, Judge Raouf contacted me. He had heard that I was also a medic and he was suffering from a very serious condition of stenosis in his spinal cord in his neck. He wanted to know where he could get the major surgery that he needed. I had his MRI scans and records provided and managed to establish that one the few places that could provide this complex surgery was quite near me in Southampton.

Major surgery was needed and it was arranged to bring Judge Raouf over for treatment. Surgery was one thing but providing all-round care for him and his family was something else. I remembered that I did have two friends near there: Elaine and Brian in Portsmouth. What's more, Brian even had links to the Kurds. I asked Brian for his help caring for the Kurdish judge who had sentenced Saddam to death. The service Brian provided was phenomenal. Not only was every aspect of the judge's needs provided for, Brian provided for all the needs of the large local Kurdish community. To such an extent that there was even a memorial to the people of Halabja killed by Saddam. The judge himself was originally from Halabja. Brian met his needs like nobody could have ever thought possible.

Brian and I returned to Kurdistan with the judge after his surgery. That was just one of many, many visits. Brian was a hero and we loved him and always will. Brian became one of our trustees and a very special one; he was the only one who had been on the ground wherever we worked. He so loved his dear wife Eileen, who he described as the greatest gift G-d had given him.

Brian, you will rest in peace and rise in great glory.

JERUSALEM MERIT (MIDDLE EAST RECONCILIATION INTERNATIONAL)

Our work and ministry is very diverse and exciting. Our title Jerusalem MERIT (Middle East Reconciliation International) describes the nature of our work.

MINISTRY AND EDUCATION

At the heart of our work, we are dedicated to ministry and education. From the education level we are involved in everything for the education of young children, having a school for Iraqi refugee children in Jordan serving hundreds of children from the age of four to eighteen. The school is predominantly Aramaic and Arabic speaking, with English being the third language. All of the pupils originally come from Iraq and their time in Jordan is just transitional until they are offered a permanent home with refugee status. Most people are moved to Australia or Canada. We have been very encouraged to see how well our children have developed, some of whom are now in university and some even studying medicine.

RELIEF AND RECONCILIATION

Another major aspect of our work is academic research and teaching. I have written twenty-six books, and there are more on the way. I regularly teach at universities in the UK and abroad. We are about to resume the Jerusalem International School of Reconciliation Studies, which I also direct.

A very exciting aspect of our work is the ongoing development of our work and ministry with the Bethel School of Supernatural Ministry in Redding, California. It is very exciting to see how our reconciliation ministry has become increasingly linked to supernatural ministry.

MEDICAL AND DENTAL

Our medical and dental clinic used to provide a very comprehensive health and dental service to all our community. Sadly, our funds were greatly reduced because of the pandemic and my long-term hospitalisation. We hope and pray we may indeed be able to reopen as soon we raise more funds. I am sure we will soon.

MY SPIRITUAL CHILDREN

MY FULLA

I have to be careful in what I say about my spiritual children. When I speak of them I always suggest that this is the person I love the most. Well, the fact is, I have loved my Fulla the longest out of all my spiritual children. She became my best friend when she was a tiny little girl. She was one of the first children to start attending St George's Anglican Church after it reopened following Operation Iraqi Freedom in 2003.

Fulla was just a tiny little girl when I first fell in love with her. I used to walk around the church courtyard with her on my shoulders. The children in our church numbered well over six hundred. I used to get told off by people for having a group called the "inner circle" of those who were closest to me. Interestingly, the thing that distinguished the inner circle from the rest of the group was that they all came to the prayer meeting on Thursday afternoon. Fulla and the inner circle once all came to England to stay with my family and meet with my English friends, who helped support Fulla's family and many others with food and health care.

As Fulla became older she would increasingly be involved in things I did around Baghdad. At times she would also join me on parish visits. They took place surrounded by thirty-five armed soldiers and a number of armed vehicles. I can remember thinking on several occasions that this was very different from my parish visits on my bicycle in England. In addition to looking after the church I also oversaw the chaplaincy at the US Embassy. Fulla would regularly come to the embassy with me and she rapidly started to develop a number of fans there also.

It was a very sad time when I realised Fulla's family were planning to leave to go to America. Both her parents were ill and required quite serious medical treatment. I used to have as a motto: "don't you leave me, I won't leave you". The day eventually came when I had to say farewell to my darling Fulla. It was a tragic day of many, many tears.

Fulla and her family moved to Chicago where I visited regularly because of my links with Wheaton College in Illinois. After her move I continued to see her regularly, until the pandemic when, due to my four months in intensive care, I was unable to see her.

I will never forget the time when I was very seriously ill with Covid. It was fascinating that my consultant had worked with me in her young days at St Thomas' Hospital. I will never forget the day when the consultant neurologist came to see me. His name was Issa Ibrahim. He apologised to me for being a Liverpool graduate and not a Thomas's one. Then he smiled at me and said, "I was a member of your Sunday school in Baghdad until I was ten." We continued talking in Aramaic. He said, "Nobody would ever believe I am standing here in Surrey talking to one of my patients in Aramaic." So he was in the same Sunday school as my dear Fulla.

The wonderful news is that my Fulla has just enlisted in the US Army.

MARIAM

Mariam is the second youngest of my spiritual children and the only one left in Baghdad. She is stunningly beautiful. I have been away from Iraq since 2014 but Mariam is the spiritual child I speak to far more often than any of my other children. Being a stunning young person I am already beginning to think about finding her the right husband. That was very much the role of the Abuna. I have always taken this role very seriously; I have very clear rules. The man must not just be a classical Christian, he must be a true believer and also speak Aramaic. It has worked several times before and I am sure it will do so again.

SARA

Sara is the sister of my ninth godchild, Hana-Rivkah. Sara is the godchild of my wife Caroline. I feel rather sorry for Sara as I have always spoilt her sister. Sara is my faithful Facebook friend. She always follows my news and passes it on to her mother, who is a very good friend of mine. She regularly comes to see me and I love her very much. Sara, are you prepared to become my spiritual child? I only have eight spiritual children, unlike my sixty godchildren.

ANGEL

My Angel is the youngest of my spiritual children at only thirteen. She lived in Pakistan where her family endured intense persecution. In recent months they have moved to Malaysia whilst her father has been in America for three years, going through the long process of trying to get his family visas to emigrate there. I love her very much and talk to her very regularly.

ERAJ

My dear Eraj is just seventeen and is also living in Karachi, Pakistan. She is the first person who ever asked me to be her spiritual father; she also calls me Dad. Eraj is my preacher girl. She is a member of both the church in Pakistan and a Pentecostal church. She regularly preaches online and has really developed an outstanding ministry of leading worship and preaching. Eraj is truly another one of my glory girls and I love her.

So as I come to the end of my journey of suffering it is a journey of glory and it is not over yet. So, this is my story, this is my song – that I will continue my journey with all my friends, little and big. The good and inspirational journey is not over yet and I love it so much.

WITHOUT GOOD FRIDAY THERE IS NO EASTER DAY

The nature of my work underwent significant changes following the pandemic, as I contracted Covid-19 and witnessed the relocation of numerous Iraqi refugees to Australia and other parts of the world. As a result, our focus shifted from providing immediate crisis-related housing, healthcare and food assistance to our community, to the challenge of supporting our people as they settled into long-term permanent residences in unfamiliar territories. Previously, most Iraqi refugees would temporarily move to Jordan or Turkey before eventually resettling in America or Canada, but in recent years, a majority of the refugees have been relocating to Australia.

I recently returned from my first visit to Australia, which proved to be an immensely emotional experience. It had been as long as seven years since I had last seen many of my beloved people, and our reunion was filled with overwhelming displays of love and joy. A key element of any Iraqi gathering is our shared mealtime, and upon my arrival, we celebrated with a remarkable feast. Over 60 people who are now in Australia attended this grand party, and it was remarkable to realise that among them were eight couples whom I had married, twelve children whom I had baptised, and over a dozen individuals whom I had guided through their first communion. This profoundly inspiring encounter allowed me to recognise that our familial bond within the kingdom is not merely momentary but eternal, a supernatural relationship.

It was fascinating to observe that the long-standing small disputes between different factions within our church continued even after years of coexistence. Equally interesting was the realisation that people still perceived me as their Abouna (spiritual father) in the same manner as when I resided among them. One of the most fulfilling aspects of my role as the spiritual leader of my congregation was the responsibility of arranging marriages for the many young women who regarded themselves as my daughters. Upon reuniting with them, one of the foremost inquiries from the community revolved around the prospects of their marital unions.

Nowadays, Christians of Iraqi descent in our community no longer identify themselves as Christians but rather as Assyrians. Remarkably, the Assyrians, who were once considered wicked during the Babylonian era, have now embraced Christianity. It is intriguing to explore the time line of when the Assyrians began their journey as followers of the G-d of Abraham, Isaac and Jacob. This transformation seems to be closely tied to what I often refer to as the arrival of the evangelist in a submarine to Nineveh. It was after Jonah's visit and proclamation of the gospel that the wicked Assyrians started returning to the faith of our forefathers.

One of the initial events we attended in Canberra, the capital of Australia, was a captivating conference titled *"Faith and Freedom under Fire,"* organised by the influential Karen Bos. Among the notable speakers at this conference was a remarkable man named Ninos, who shared with us an extensive account of Assyrian history, despite not having lived in Iraq himself. His family had been settled in Australia for several generations. I deeply valued the profound insight into Assyrian history that he provided.

Later in the month, we had the opportunity to meet the Assyrian Patriarch. Initially, when I was called to work in Iraq, I struggled with the notion that I was relinquishing my initial calling, which clearly revolved around Israel. However, Ninos's presentation brought a sense of certainty that Assyrian and Hebrew history are intertwined. This realisation was underscored by Ninos's delivery. Moreover, the incredible journey that led me from Jerusalem to Babylon ultimately resulted in the unification of the people I cherished deeply and had been called to serve. Reflecting on my own enduring trials and the sufferings endured by individuals like Emily, I have become acutely aware of the profound manner in which the glory of the Almighty accompanies us. Through the loving relationship I have cultivated with young Emily, I can honestly attest that being with her has provided some of the most awe-inspiring moments of divine splendour I have ever witnessed in my life.

Whenever I think of her, my heart overflows with love for Emily. While I grieve for her and the suffering she endured, since the time of her funeral, I am certain of the glorious presence of the Almighty, with whom our dear Emily now resides. Reflecting on the sufferings endured by myself and many others, I am acutely aware of the greatest symbol of glory that I possess: the actual Bible that belonged to the renowned revivalist, Smith Wigglesworth.

The story behind my possession of this treasure is intertwined with the early Pentecostal revivalist movement at the beginning of the last century. Smith Wigglesworth, who came from a humble background as a plumber, was a key figure in the movement. In those days, plumbing was not a respected profession, unlike today where it can be highly regarded and lucrative. My grandfather, Charlie Bishop, was among the first students of the Assemblies of God Pentecostal Bible College, which was initially located in Paddington, London, before moving to Hampstead Heath. Smith Wigglesworth frequently visited these colleges as a guest lecturer due to his shared background with my grandfather. I presume that their shared plumbing background played a role in their close friendship.

After my grandfather graduated from the Bible College, he became one of the students who travelled up north to assist Smith Wigglesworth in his ministry and travels throughout the country. The leader of the Bible school at that time was the late revivalist Donald Gee, another significant figure in the revival movement. When Smith Wigglesworth passed away in 1947, Donald Gee conducted his funeral. I believe it was because of this historic connection between Wigglesworth, Donald Gee and my grandfather that Wigglesworth's Bible was passed down to him. While my grandfather may not have been a prominent leader like the others mentioned, he played a significant role in supporting the great servant of G-d. Interestingly, Smith Wigglesworth once told my grandfather that though we may have started as simple plumbers turned preachers of the Holy Spirit, our children would become doctors who would bring physical healing to the broken. It is intriguing that both Dr Henry Fardel, Smith Wigglesworth's great-grandson, and I ended up pursuing careers in the medical profession. Dr Henry Fardel and I remain close friends to this day. When I reflect on these stories, I cannot help but delight in the immense humour that lies within the words and works of G-d.

My Wigglesworth Bible has been an integral part of my own supernatural ministry. It has accompanied me in every aspect of my life and ministry, even in the most challenging war zones. The only time I did not have the SW Bible with me was during the worst experience of my life, which was not in a war zone but in the complete isolation of the Covid Zone in the Intensive Care Unit. Even if I had been able to communicate the need for it, I couldn't have retrieved it as I was in complete and utter isolation. After months of isolation, G-d spoke to me and reassured me that even though the Bible was not physically with me at that moment, it was still waiting for me, and the abundant glory of G-d was still present, as it indeed was. Even in the isolation of the Covid Zone, G-d was there.

In recent days, I had the incredible opportunity to reunite with hundreds of Iraqi children in Australia, some of whom I hadn't seen in up to seven years. My love for them knows no bounds. The experience in Australia was unforgettable and has caused me to re-evaluate the nature of my life in light of my current circumstances.

I have come to realise that the focus of my life and ministry has undergone a radical shift. No longer am I primarily involved in addressing the urgent needs of refugees on the front lines. Instead, I am now ministering to my people in their rehabilitated state, in a place of hope and refuge. Witnessing the flourishing of my young ones in Australia was simply amazing. All those who had completed their schooling were pursuing higher education at universities, excelling in subjects related to medical sciences, including medicine and dentistry.

I express my gratitude to my G-d despite the immense suffering I have witnessed and endured, including the excruciating pain of losing my dear Emily. While her loss was deeply profound, it pales in comparison to the heartbreak experienced by Lyndsey and Paul Yeskoo. I vividly remember the day I first heard about Emily in the Embassy in Baghdad during a chapel service. When I asked the congregation who among them had been grappling with unanswered prayers, it was then that Paul Yeskoo shared about his beloved daughter Emily, who had been severely affected by a cerebral disease, rendering her quadriplegic for many years. Instantly, my heart was drawn to dear Emily, and I began visiting her in Toronto as often as possible. Despite her inability to communicate through words, I quickly discovered numerous other ways to connect with her. She could understand what I was saying, and it didn't take long for me to learn what brought her joy.

Emily had a great fondness for the colour purple, and soon she became known as Emily Purple. I had a dedicated team working with me at the time, and wherever we went, we would search for anything purple that Emily would appreciate. From purple pictures to purple clothing and wraps, we did everything to honour her love for that colour. At her funeral, almost everyone in attendance wore something purple. It was an incredibly sorrowful day, yet it also marked the triumph of Emily Purple.

As I reflect on my life and the lives of those around me, it becomes evident that it has been a life marked by profound suffering. However, amidst the immense pain that has been all too real, there has also been a glorious presence. This glory is manifested through the demonstration of the gifts of the Holy Spirit in our ministry. Signs, wonders and miracles are increasingly abundant. This ministry has truly progressed from one level of glory to another. It is crucial to recognise that there can be no glory without the cross at the centre. And there can be no cross without pain. Thus, even in the midst of suffering, true glory exists. The reality is, without Good Friday, there is no EASTER DAY.